I0443611

GRAYSCALE COLORING BOOK FOR ADULTS:

WILD ANIMALS

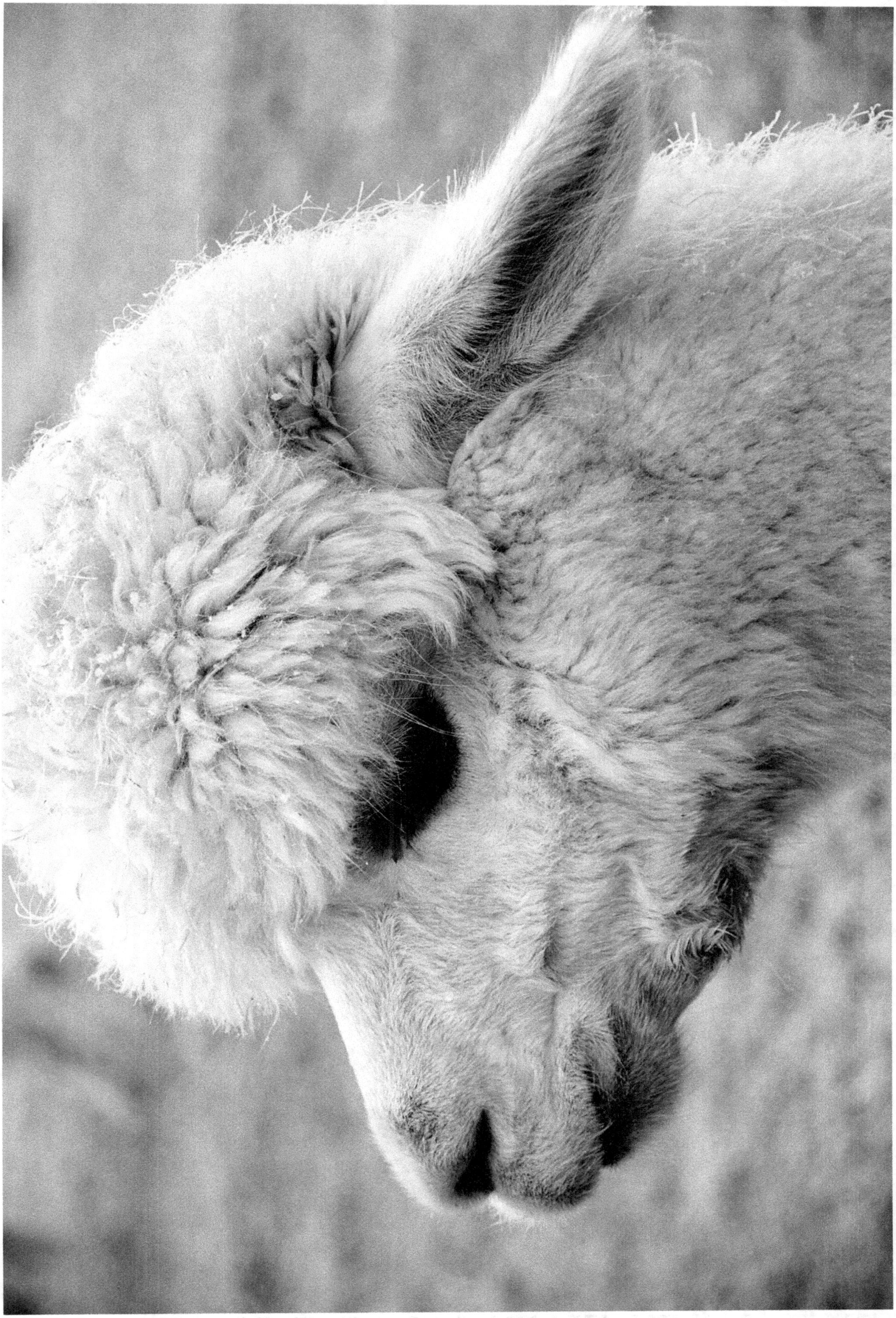

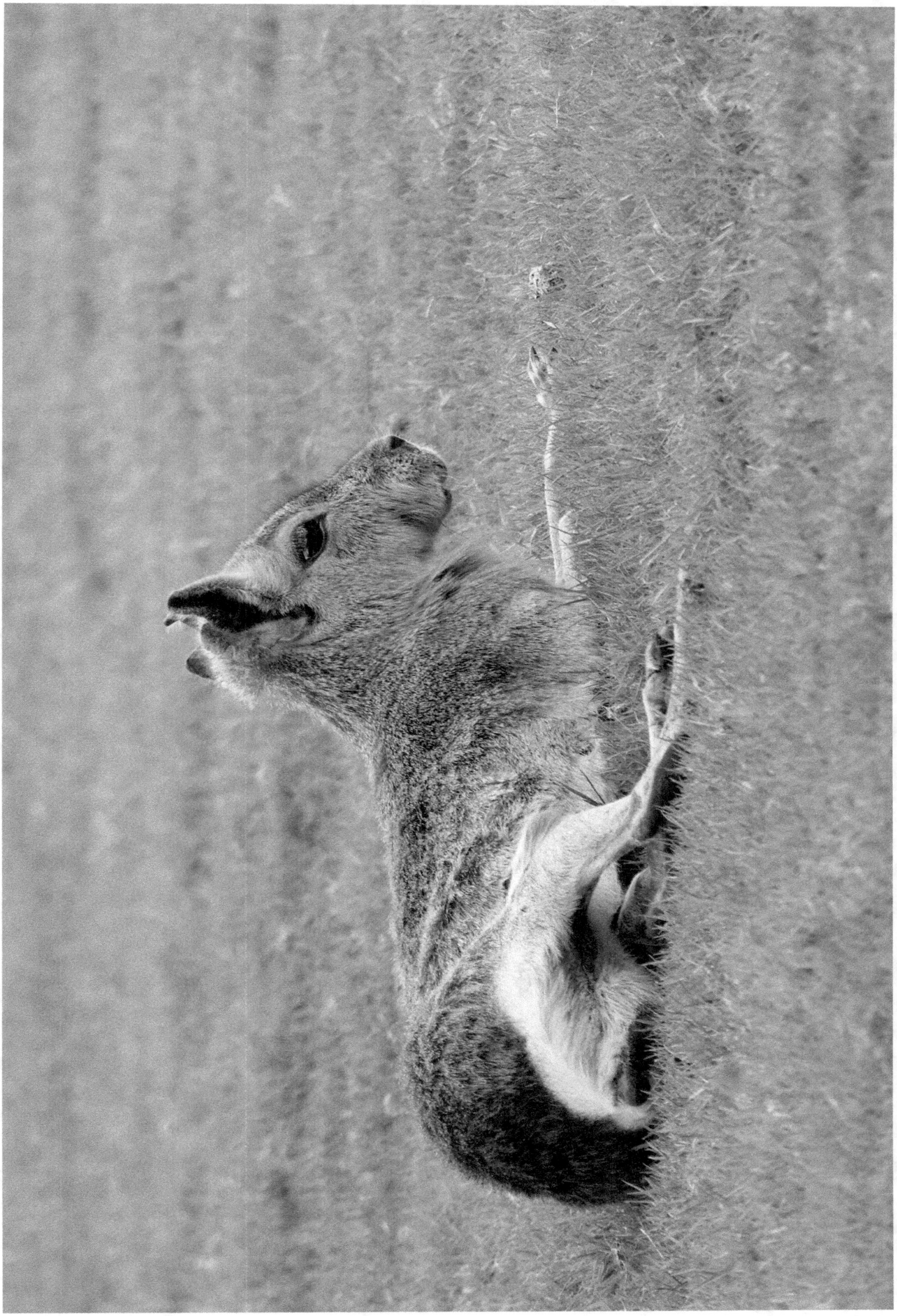

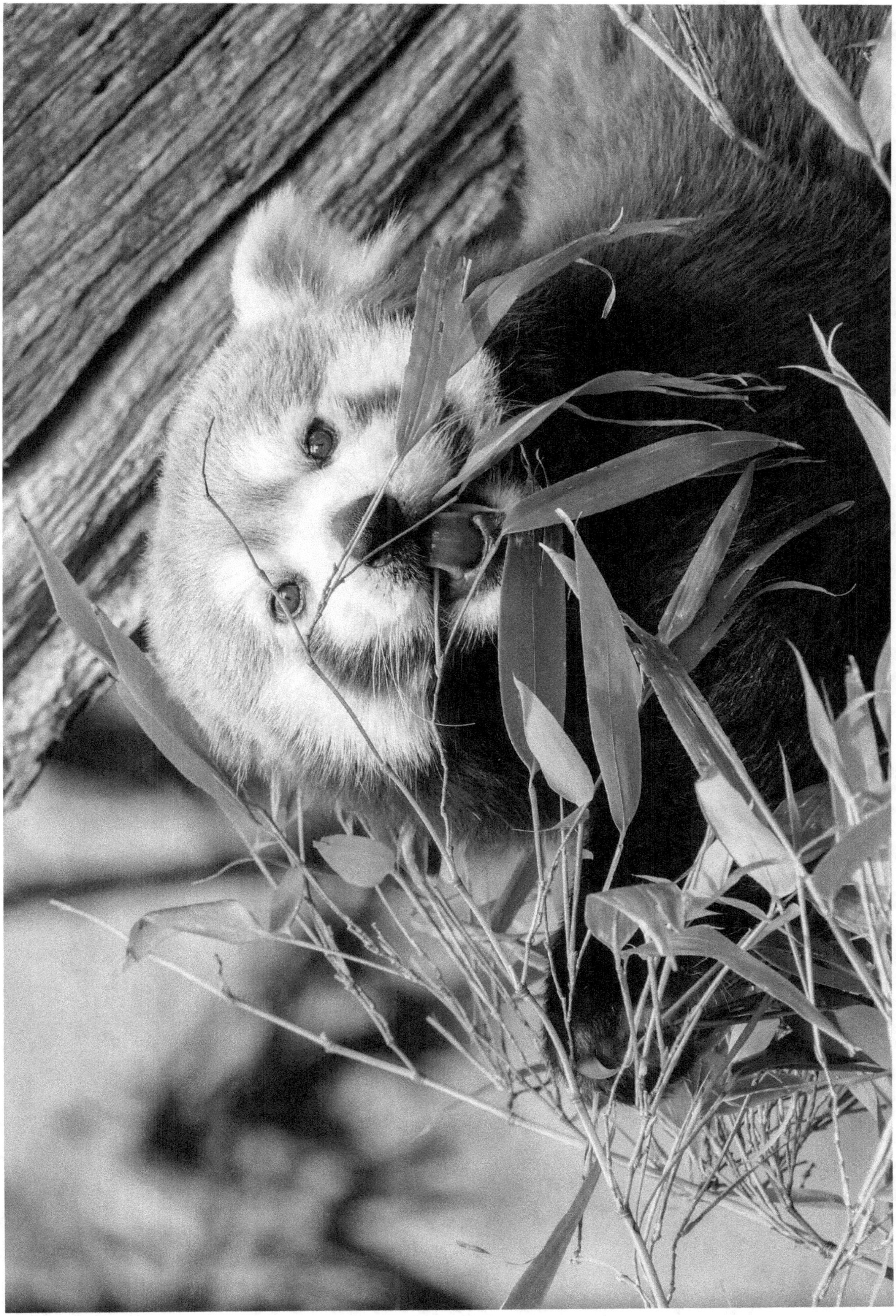

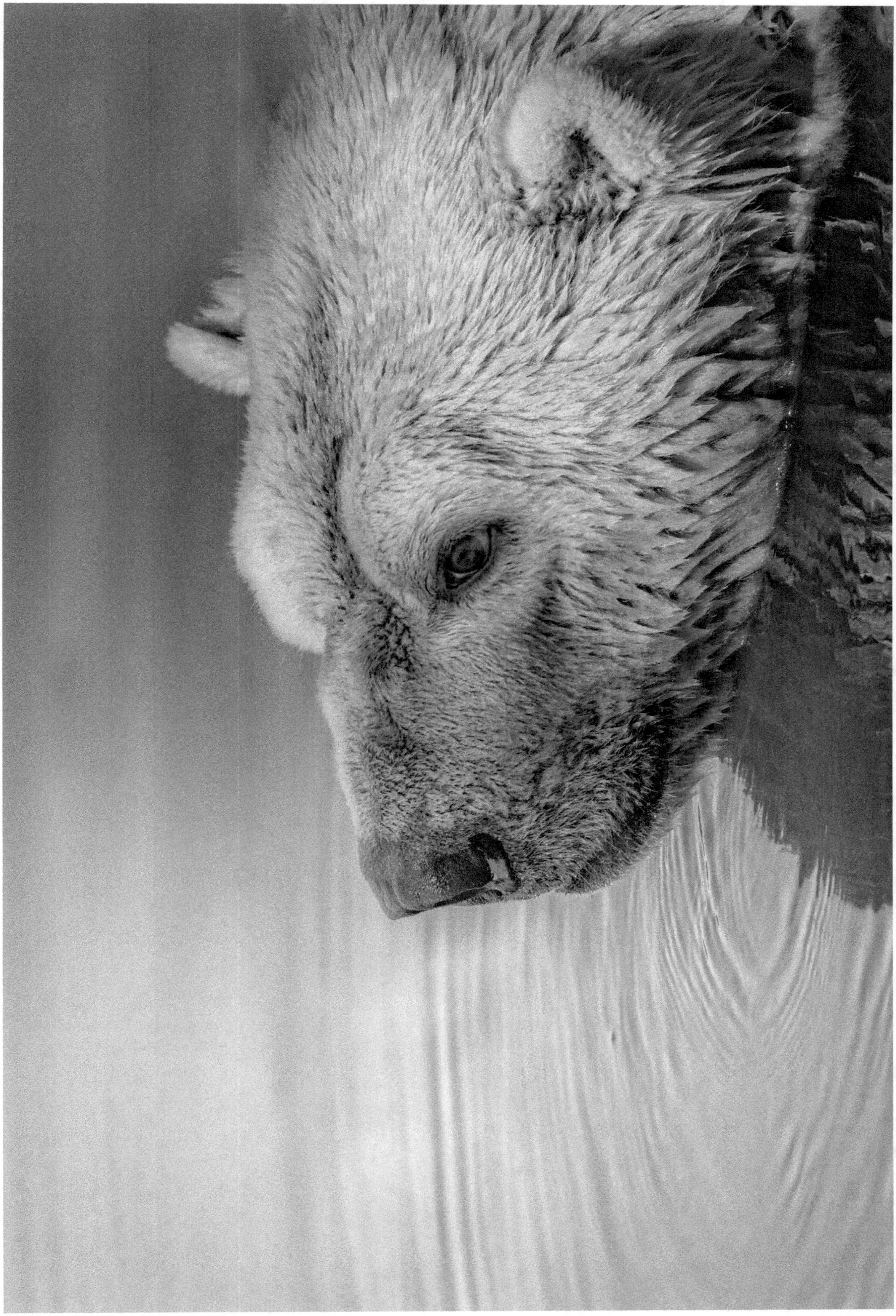

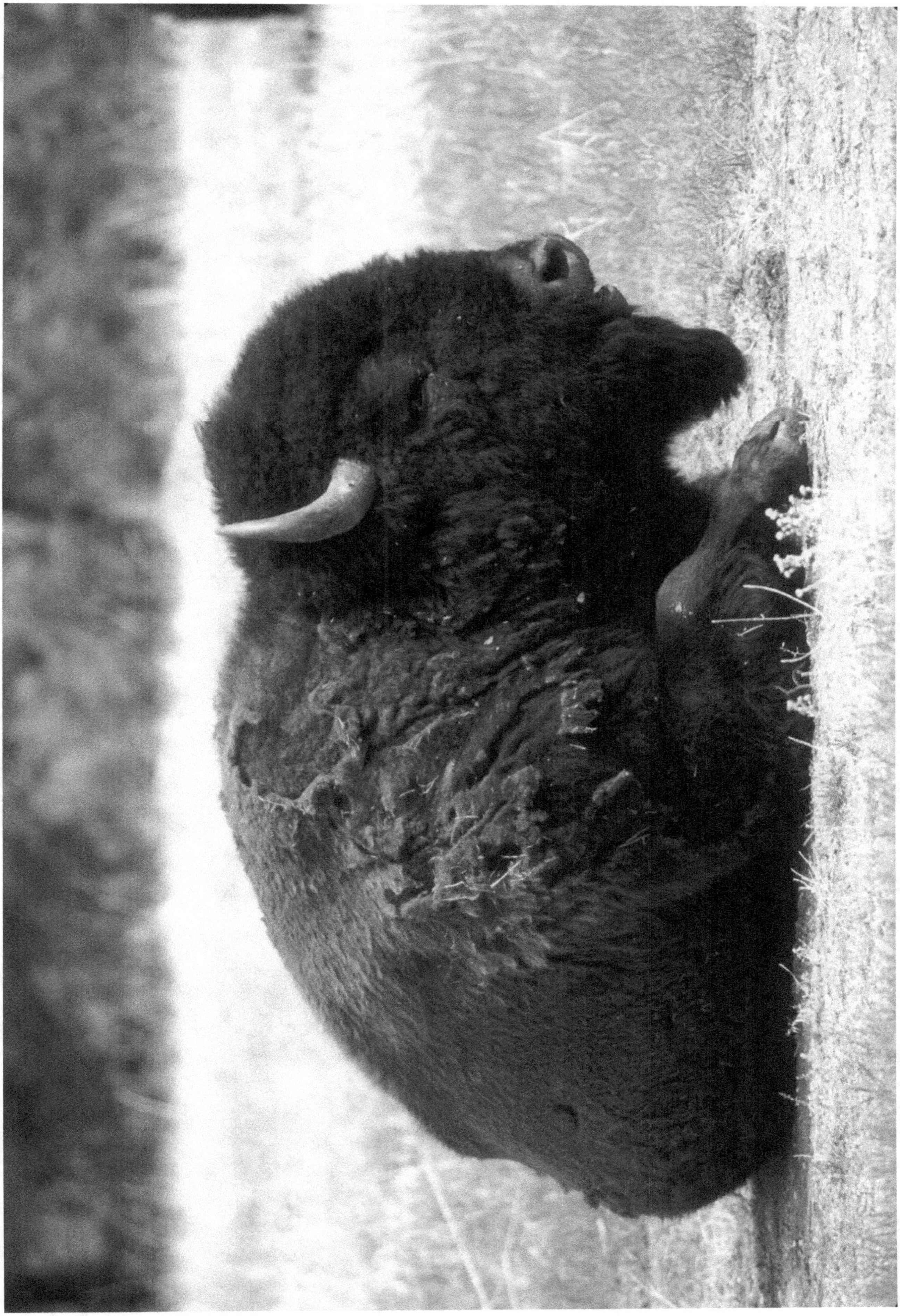

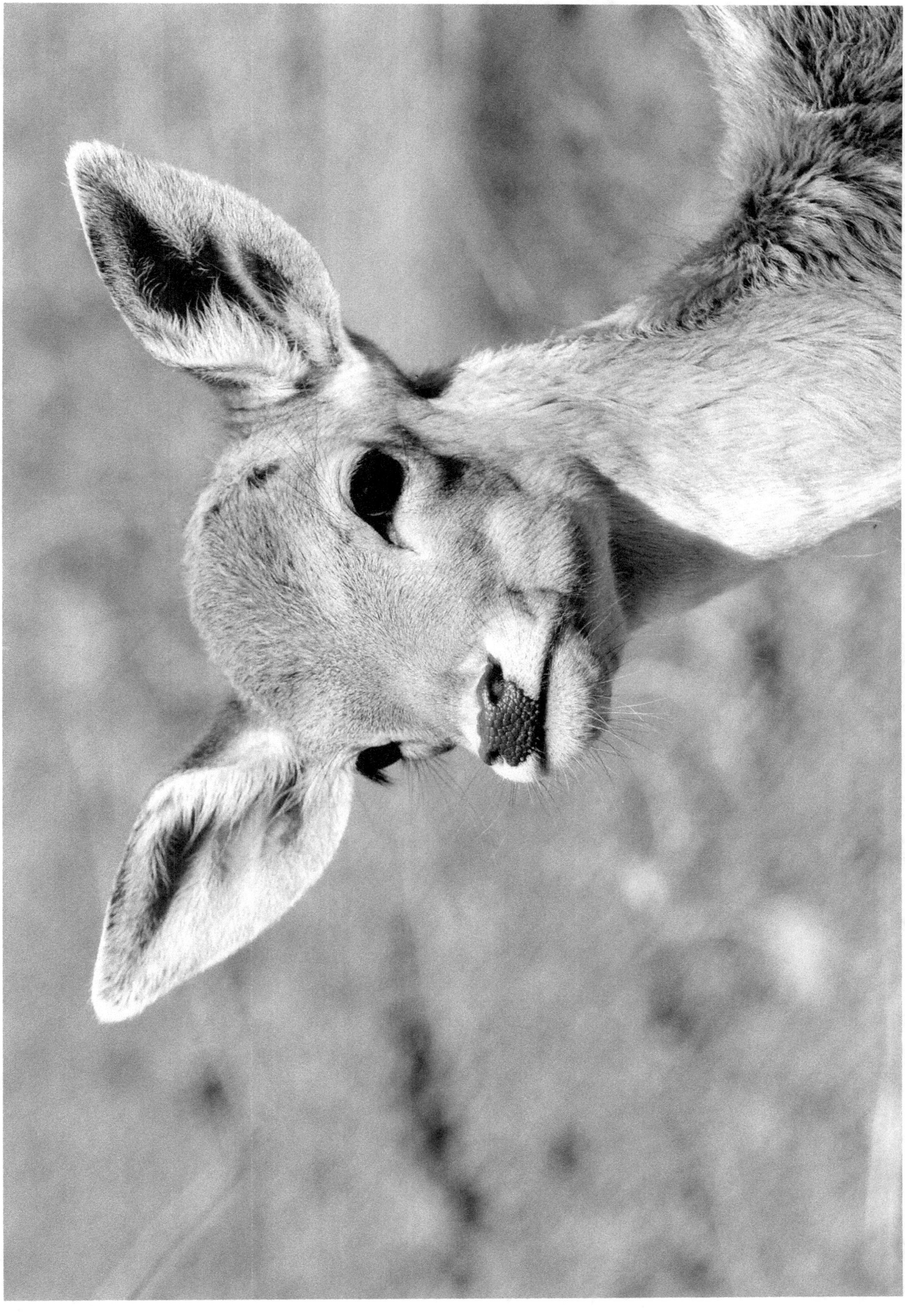

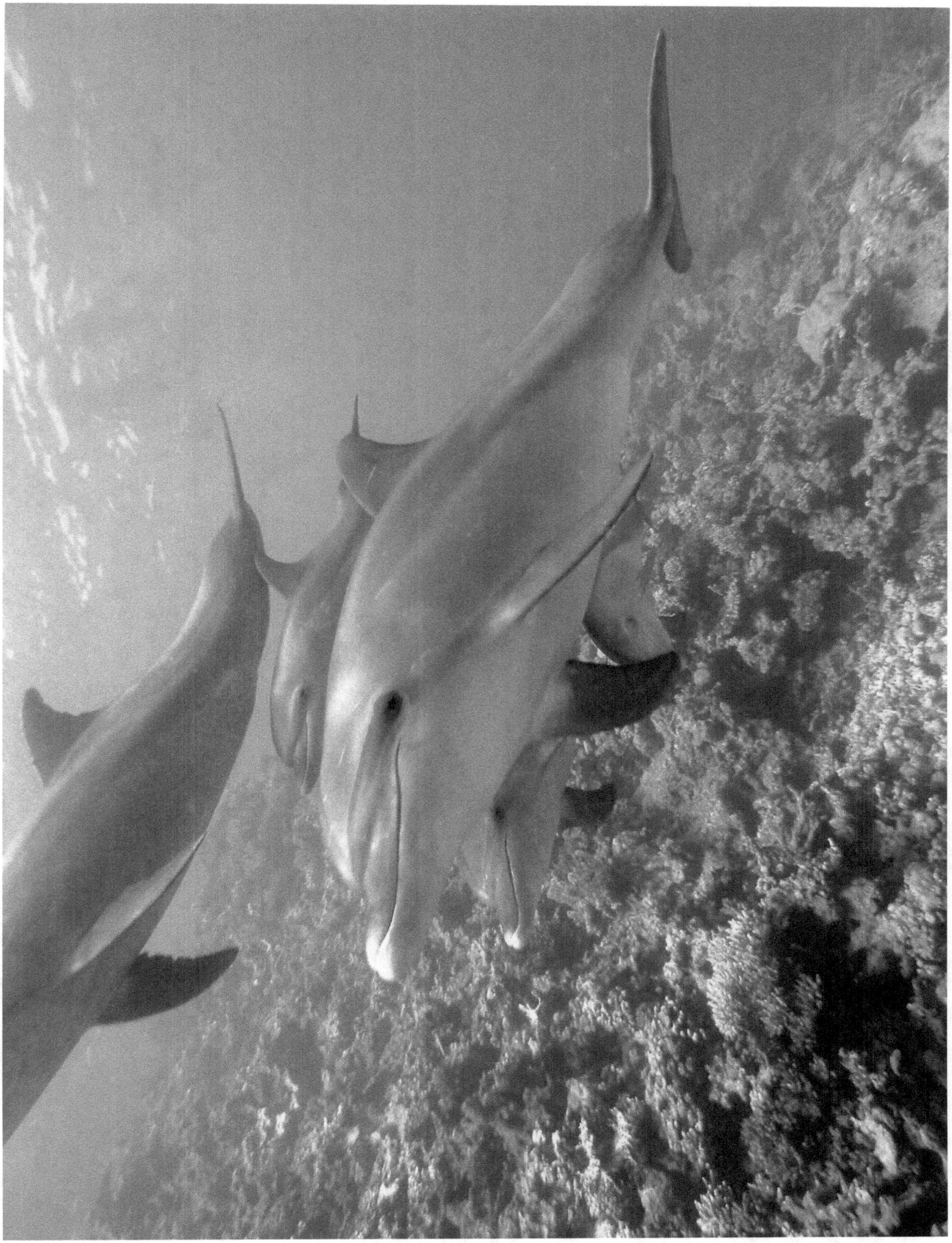

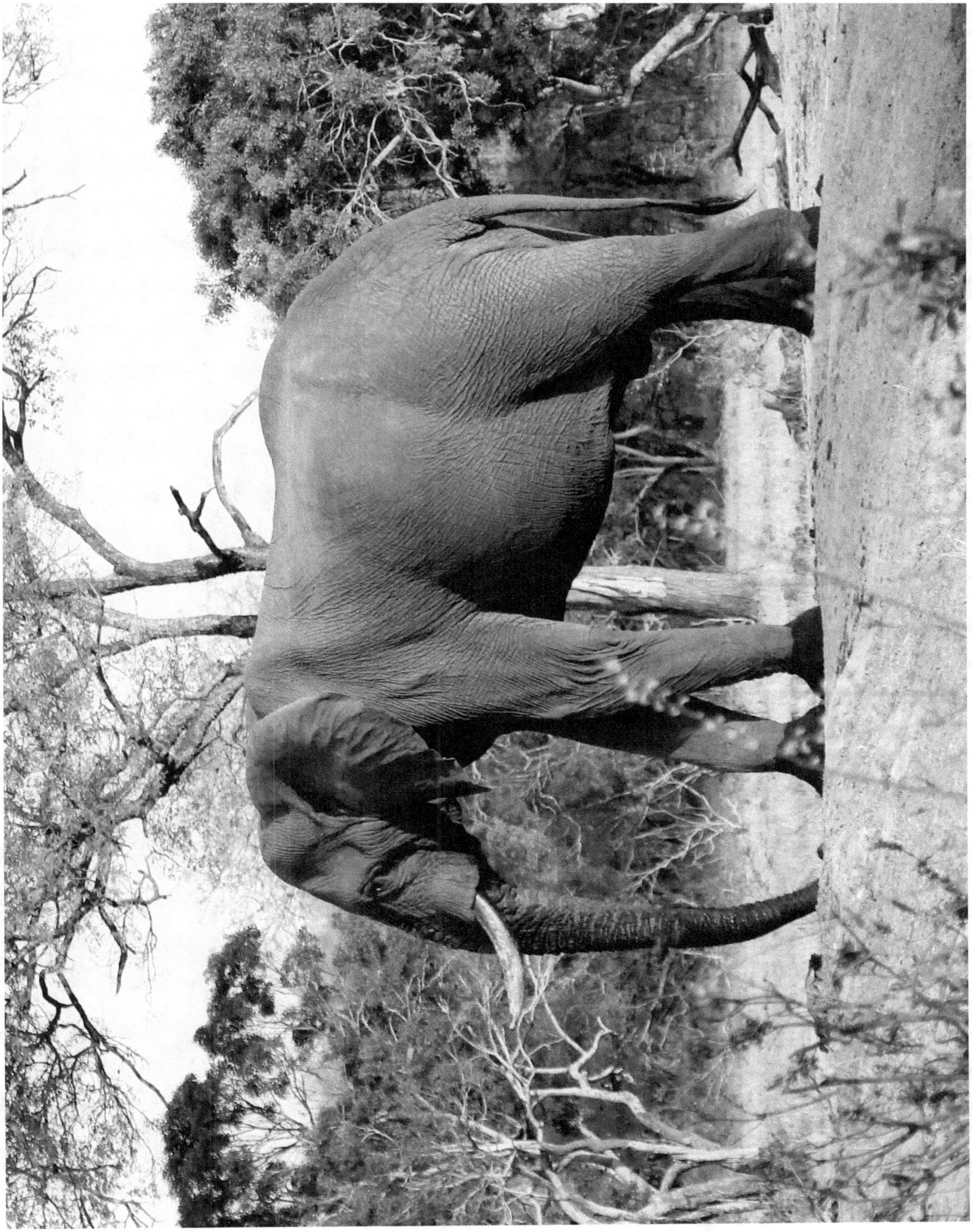

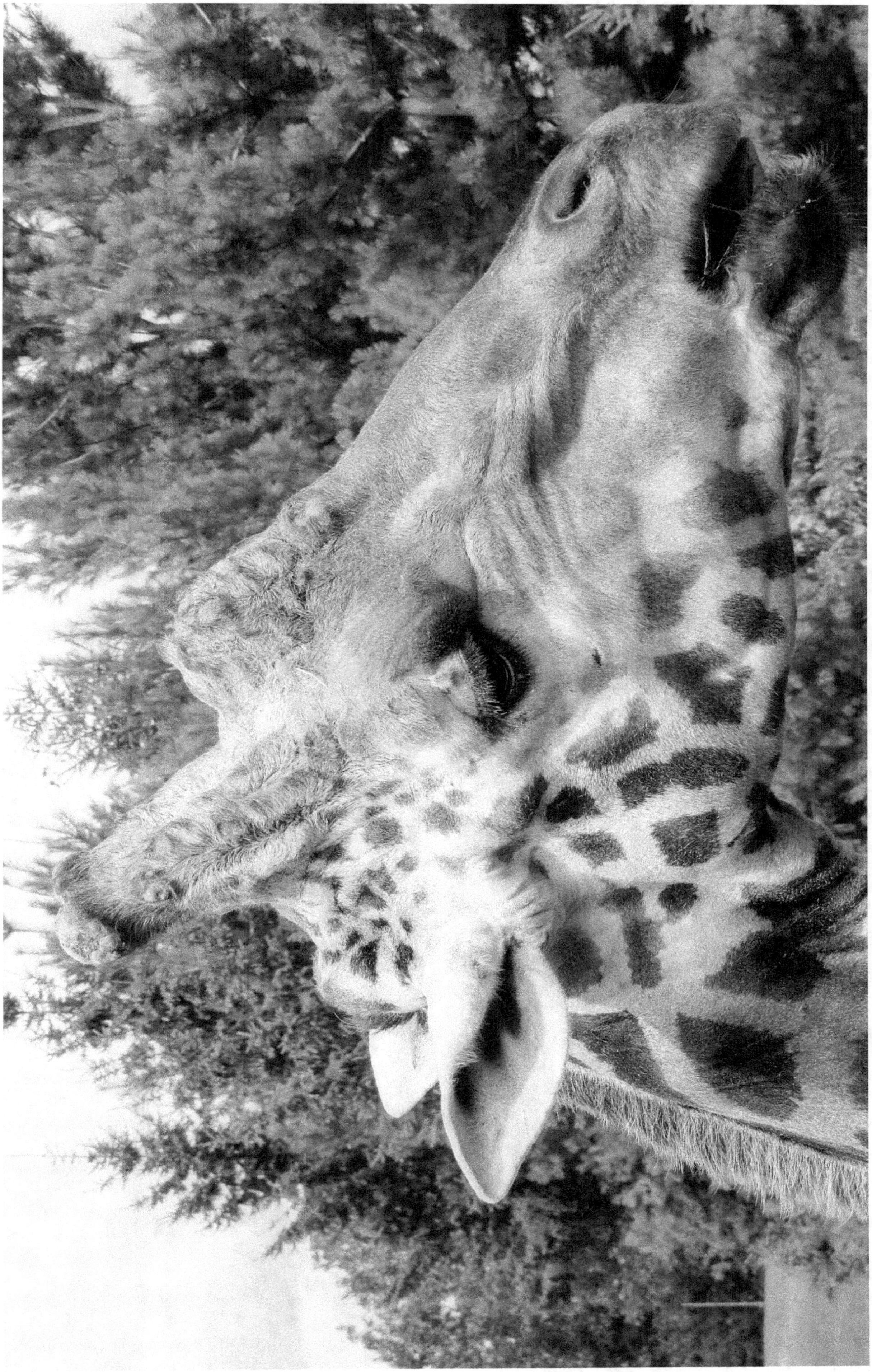

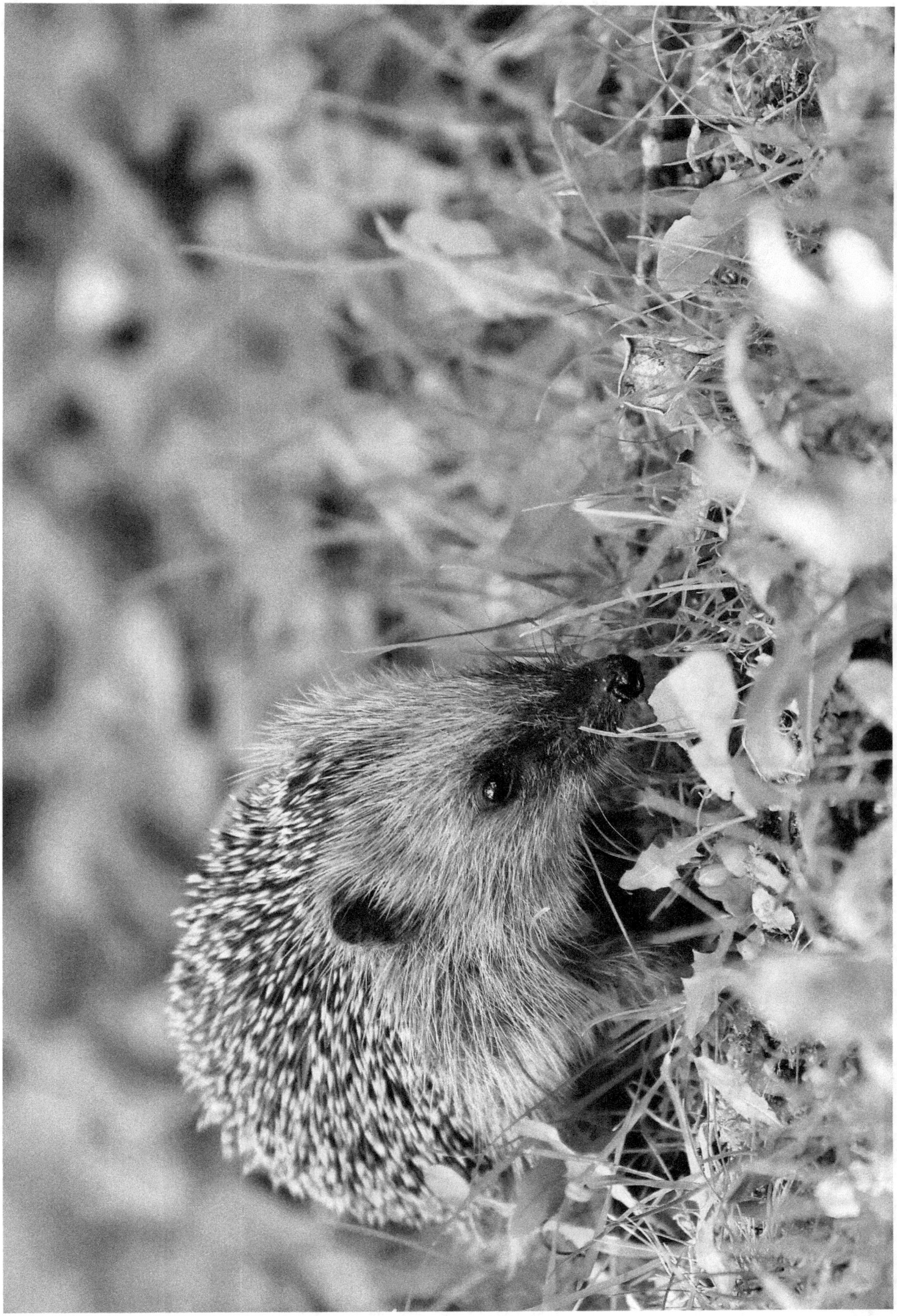

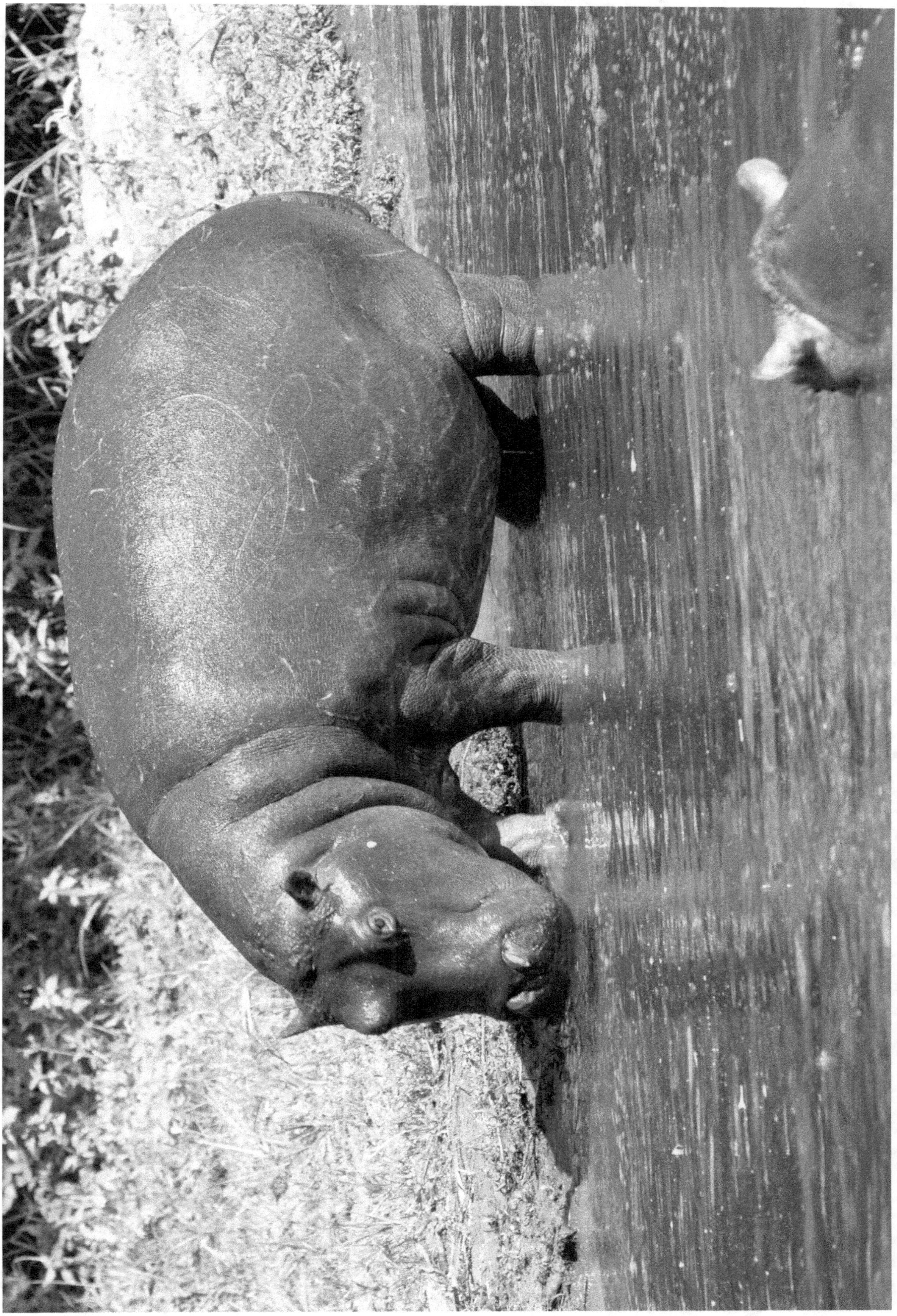

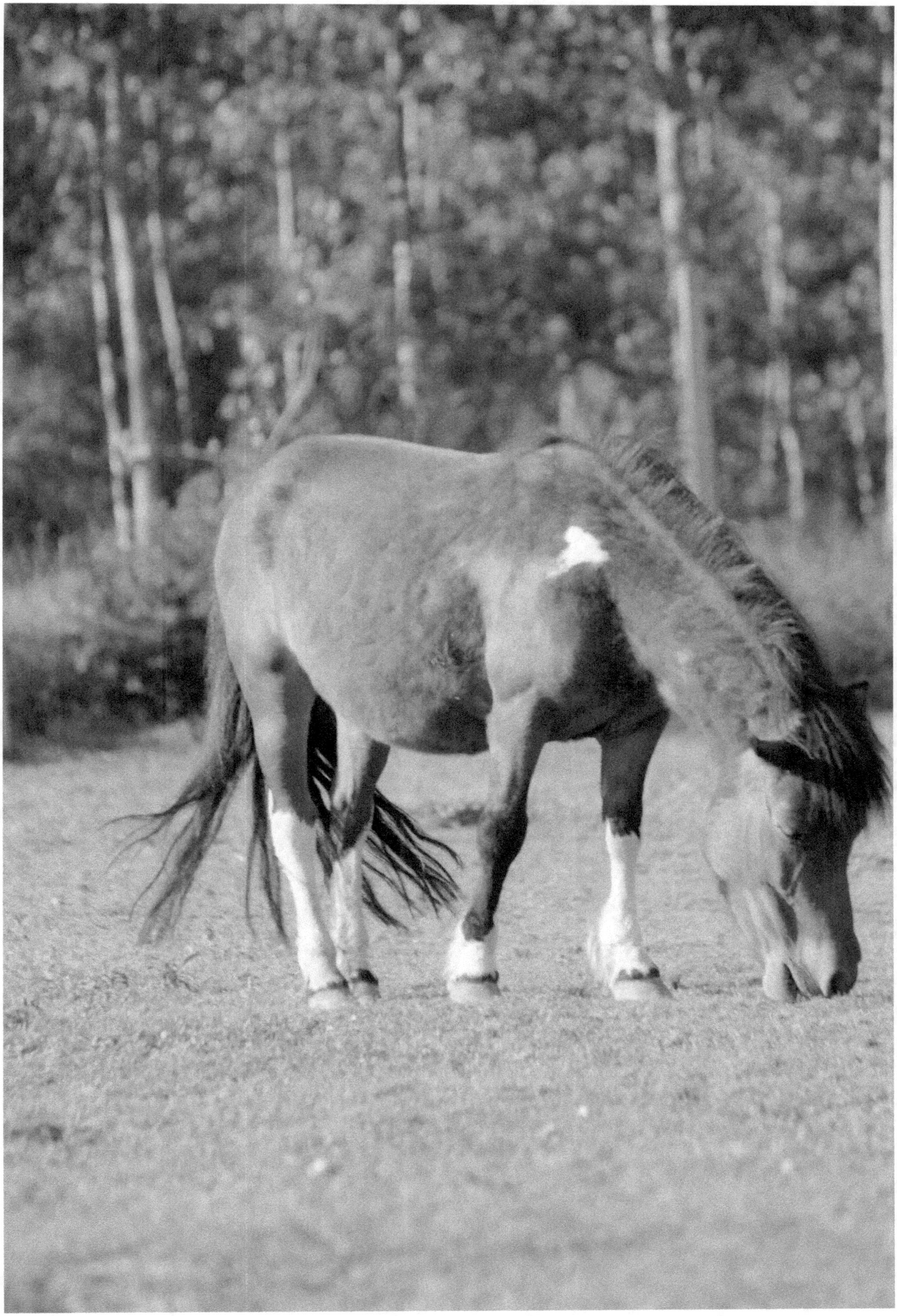

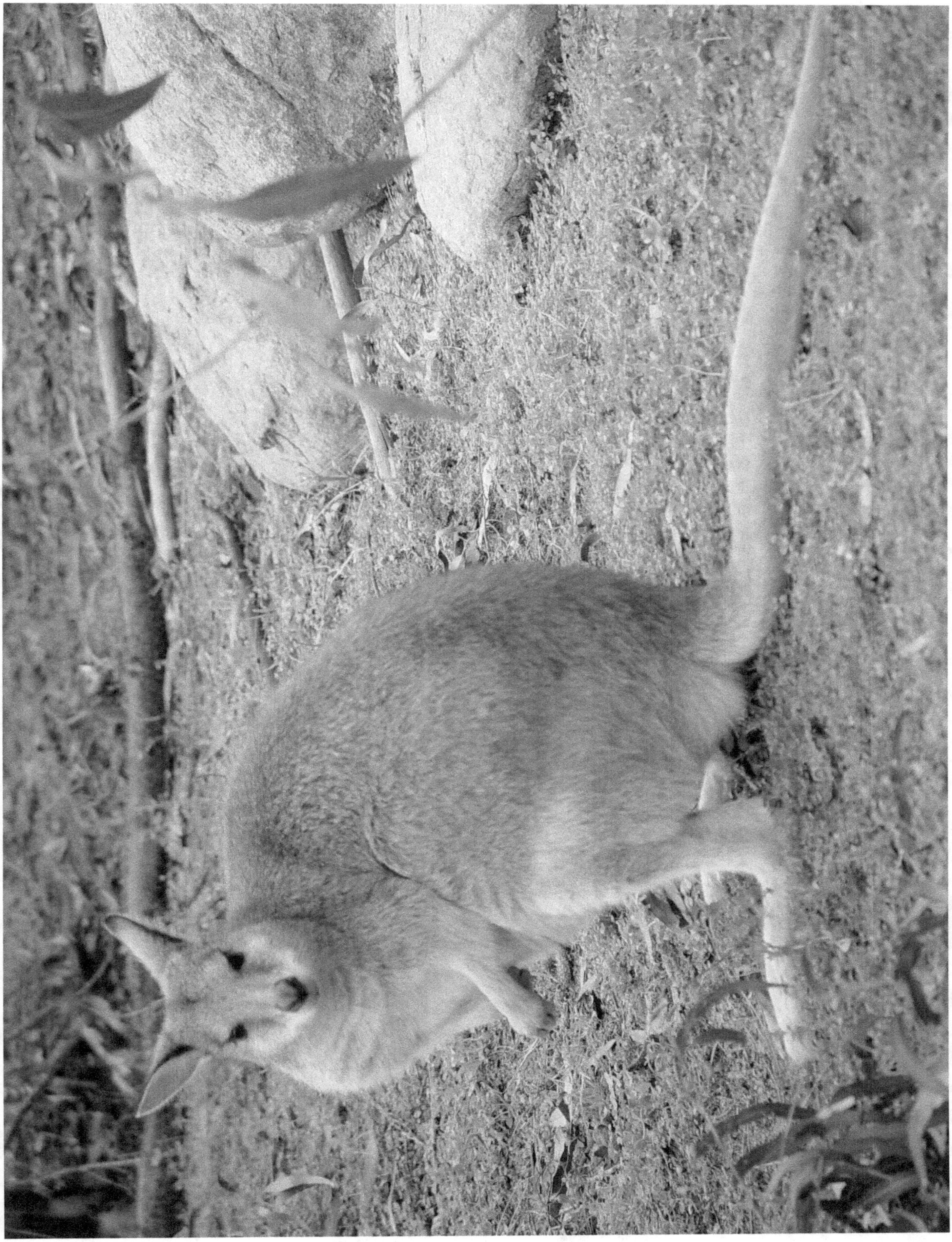

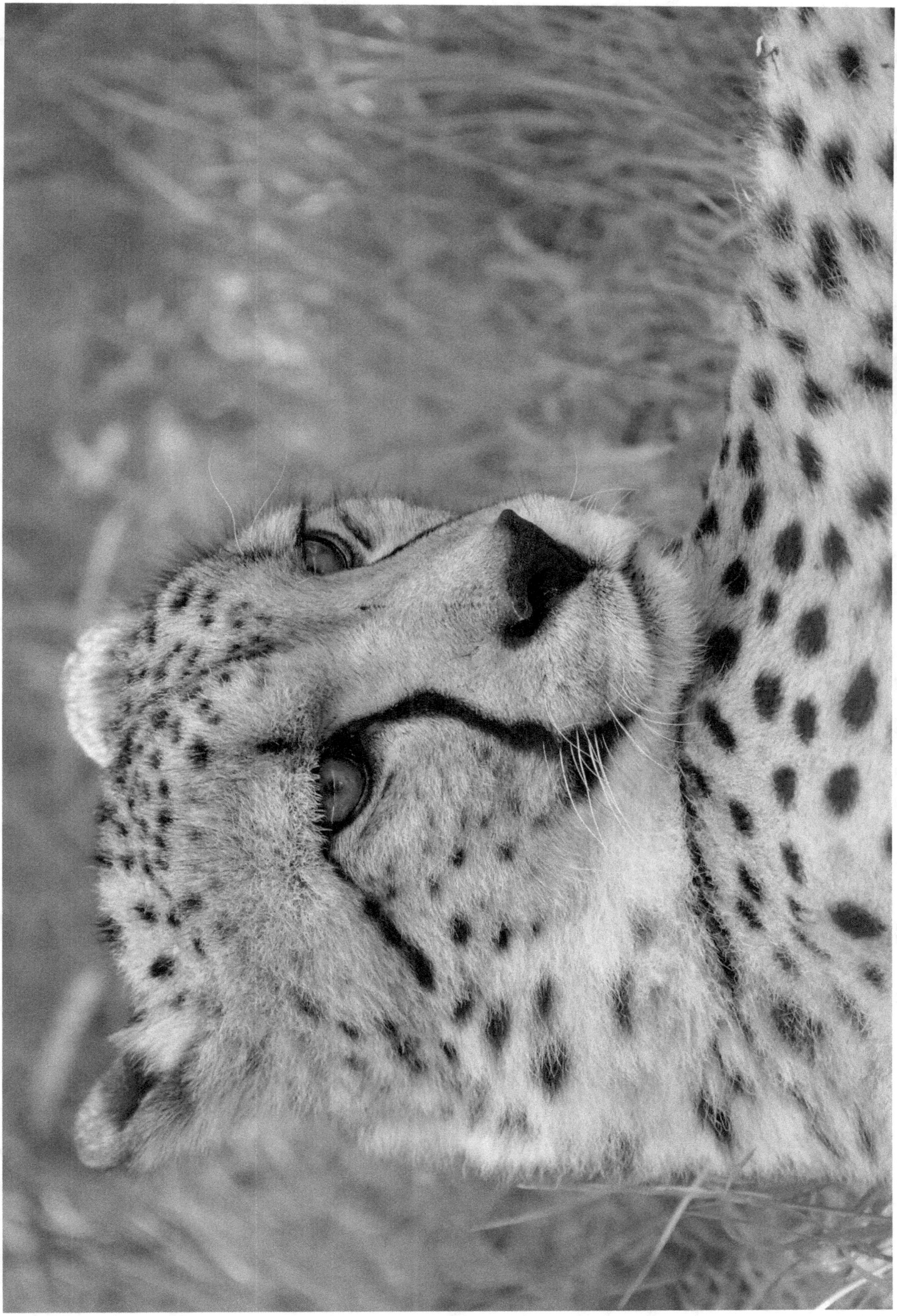

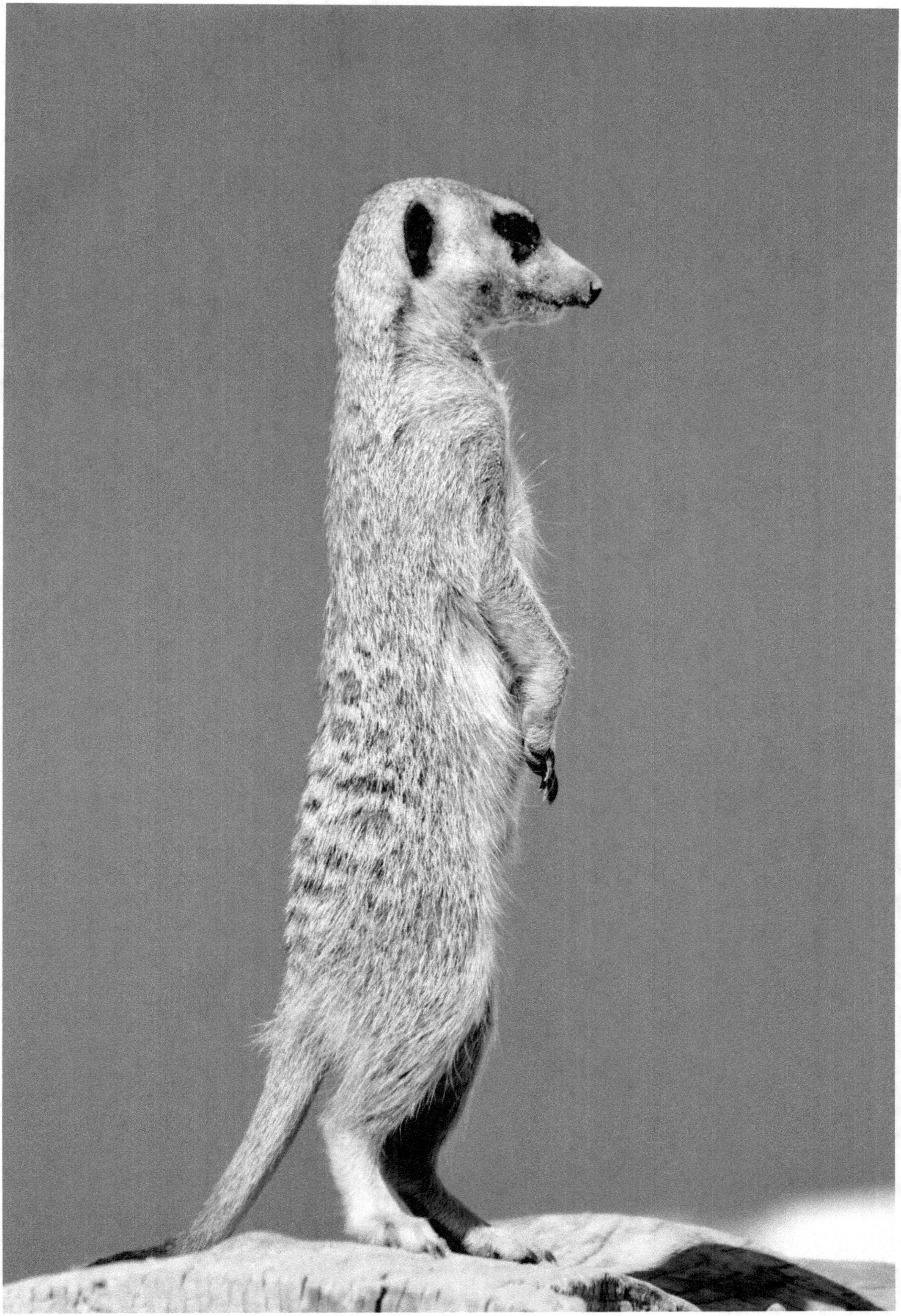

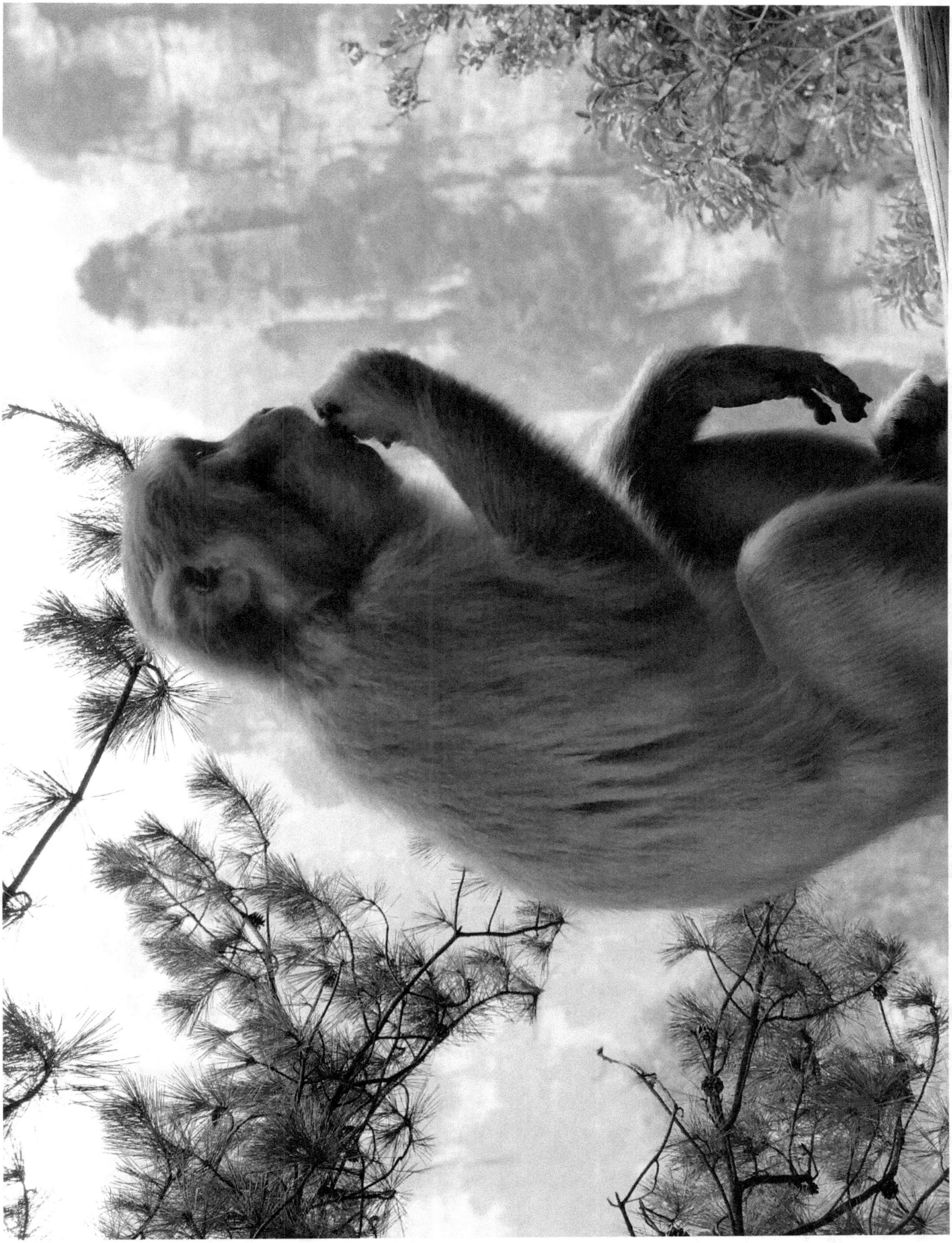

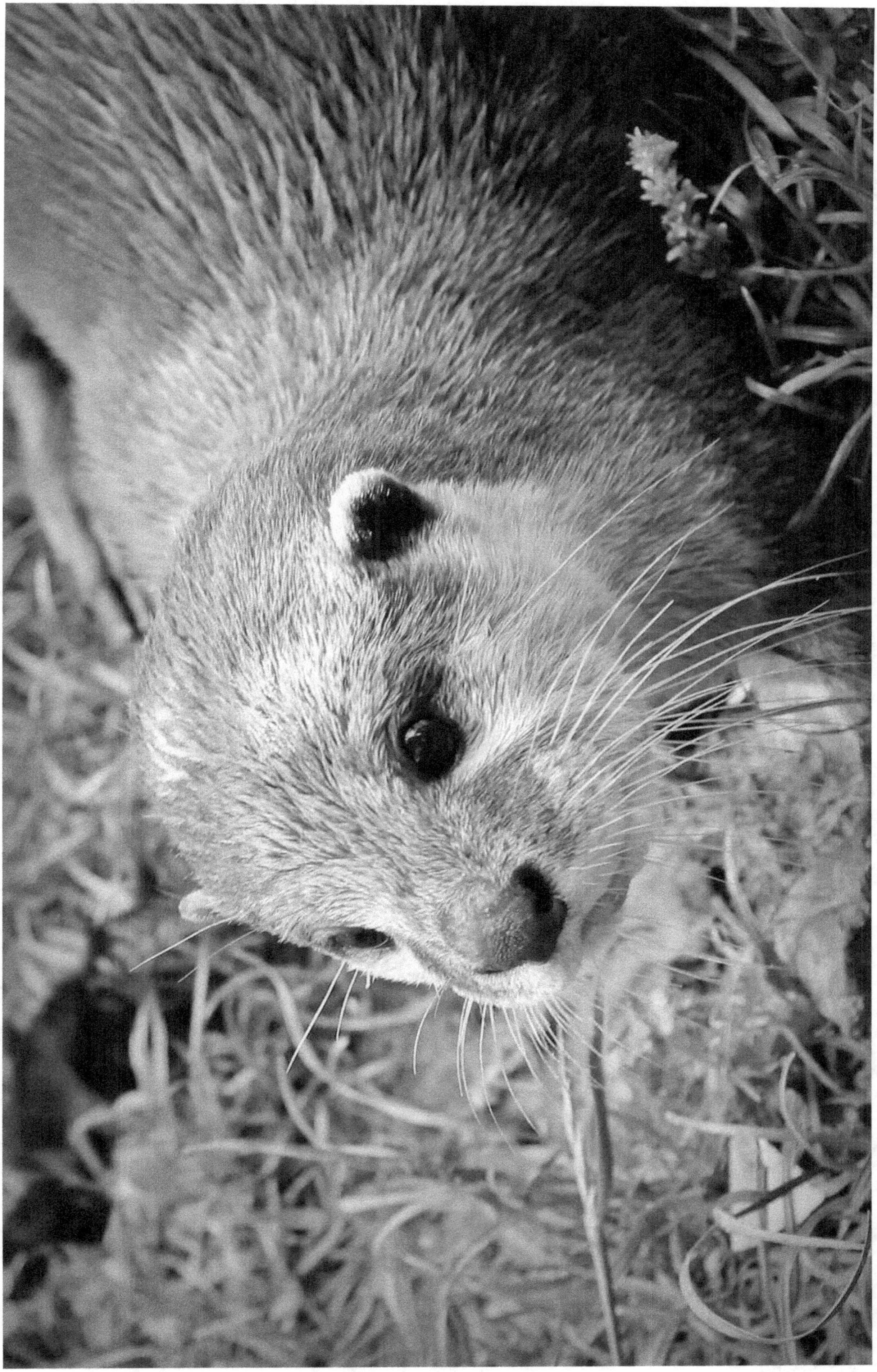

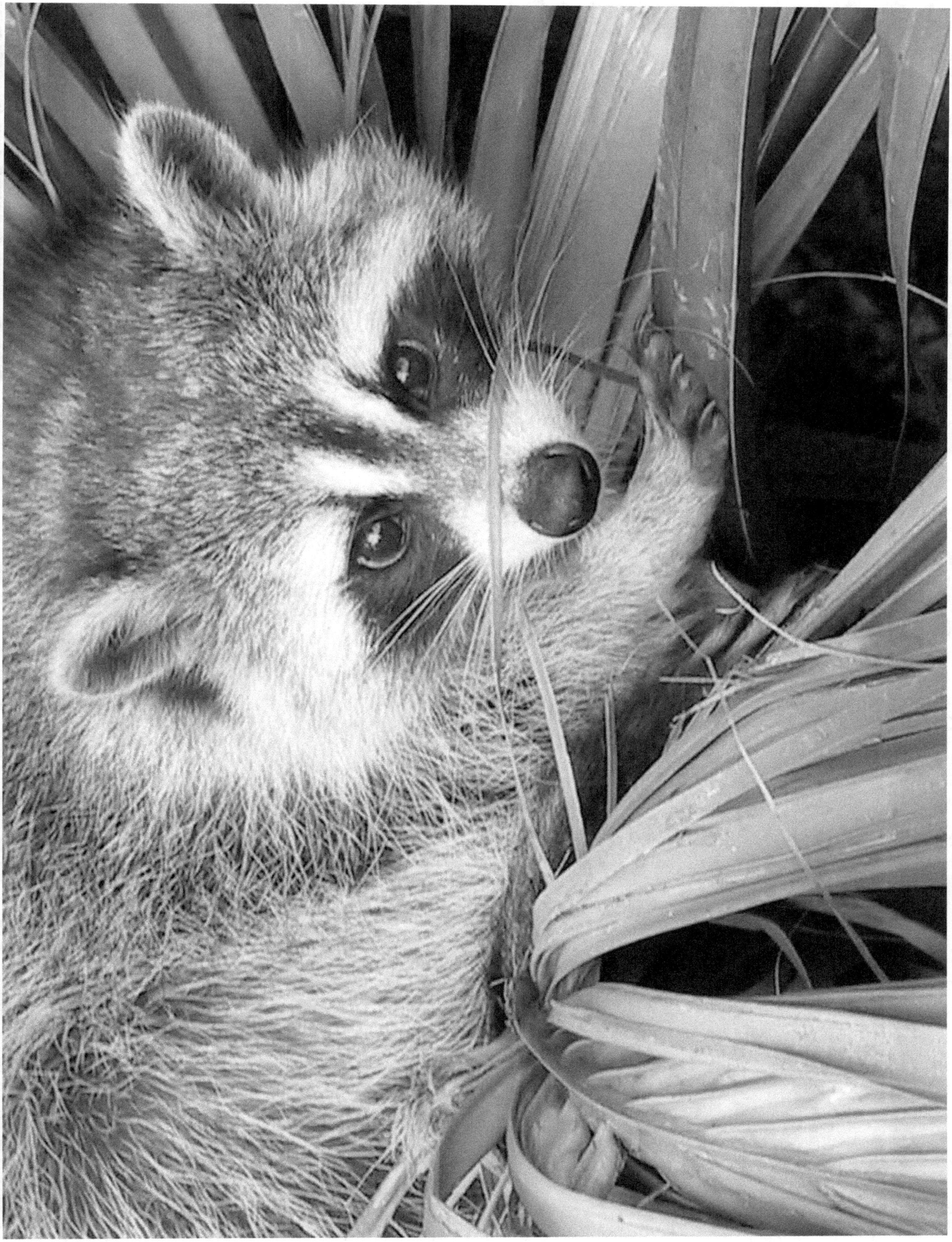

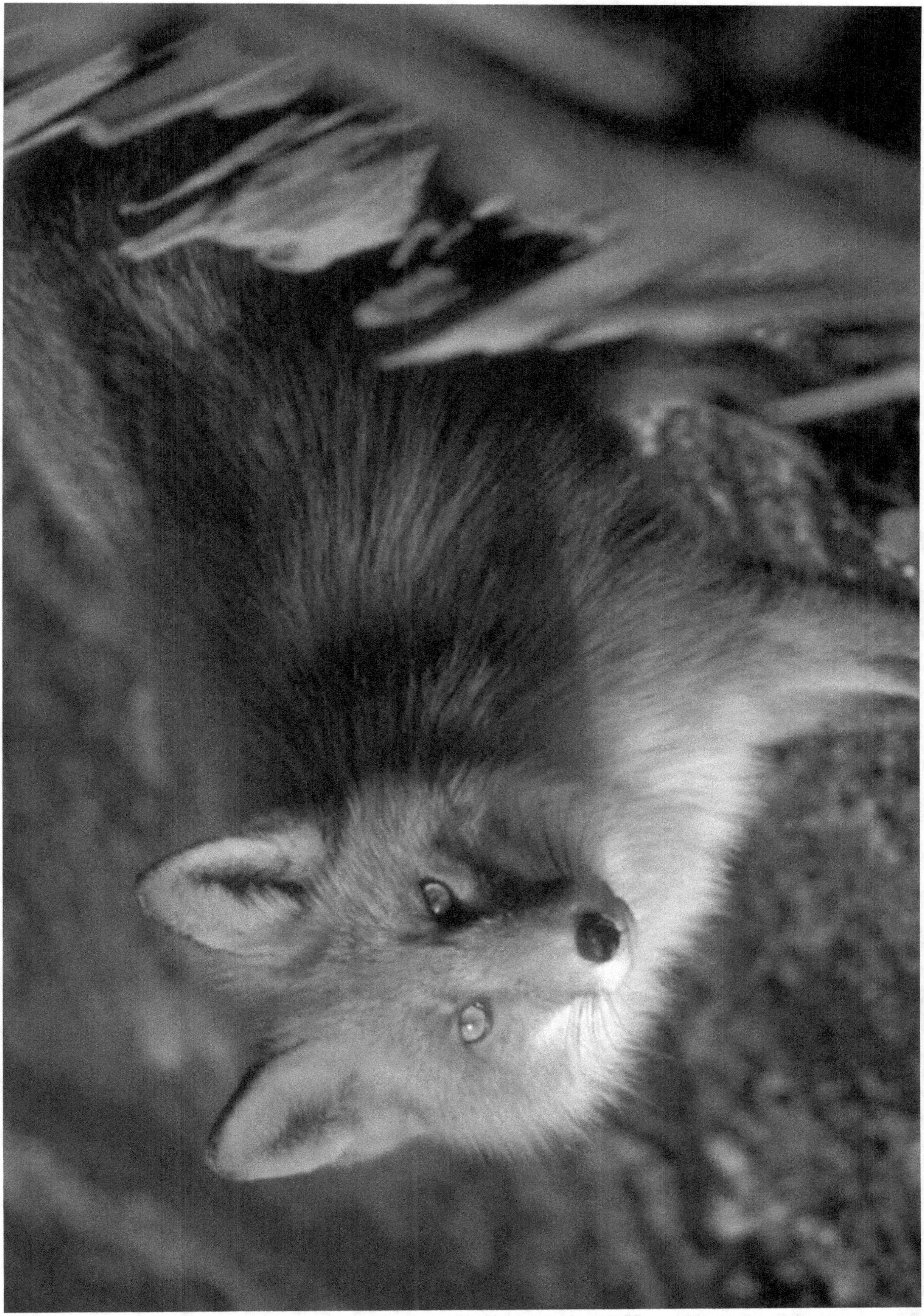

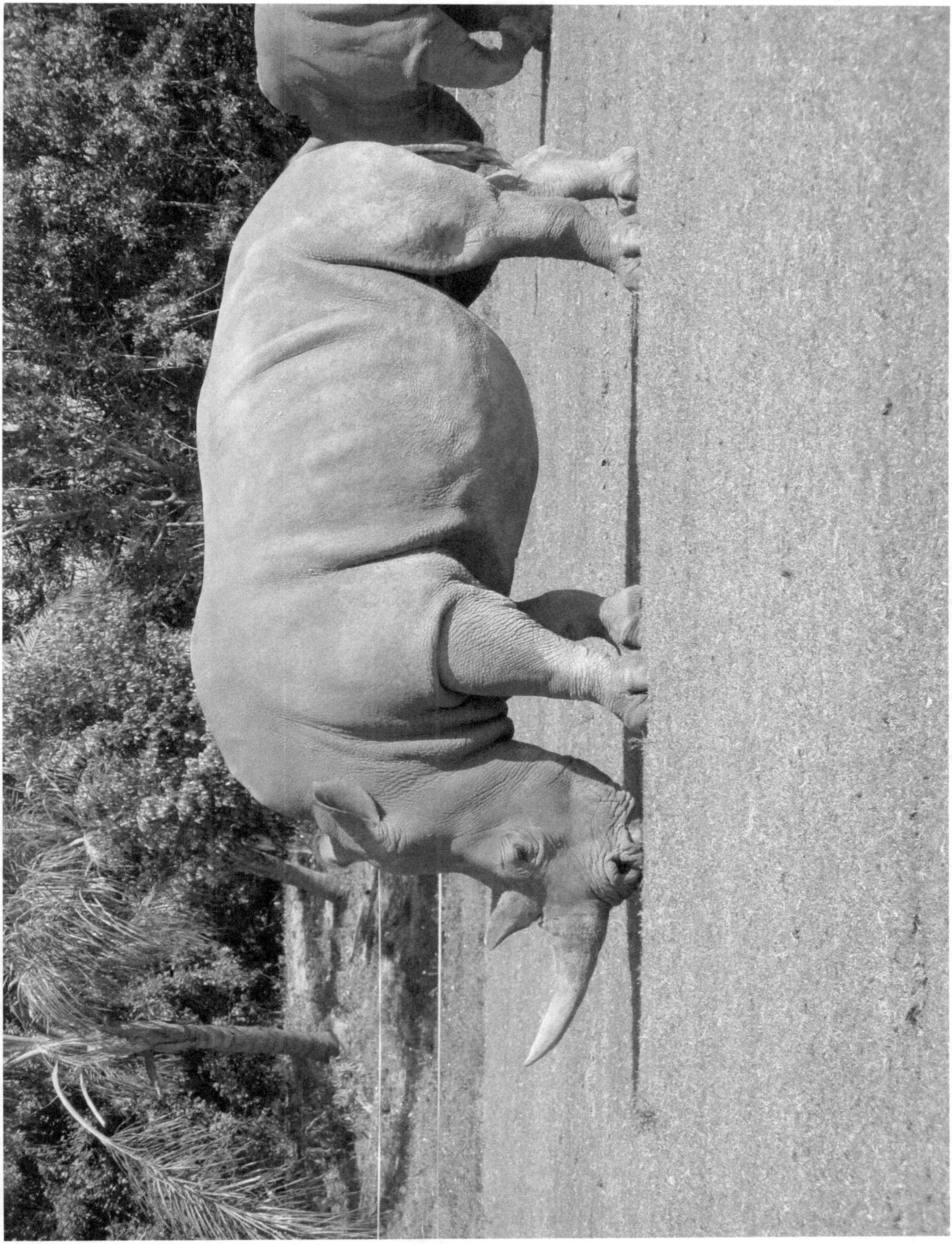

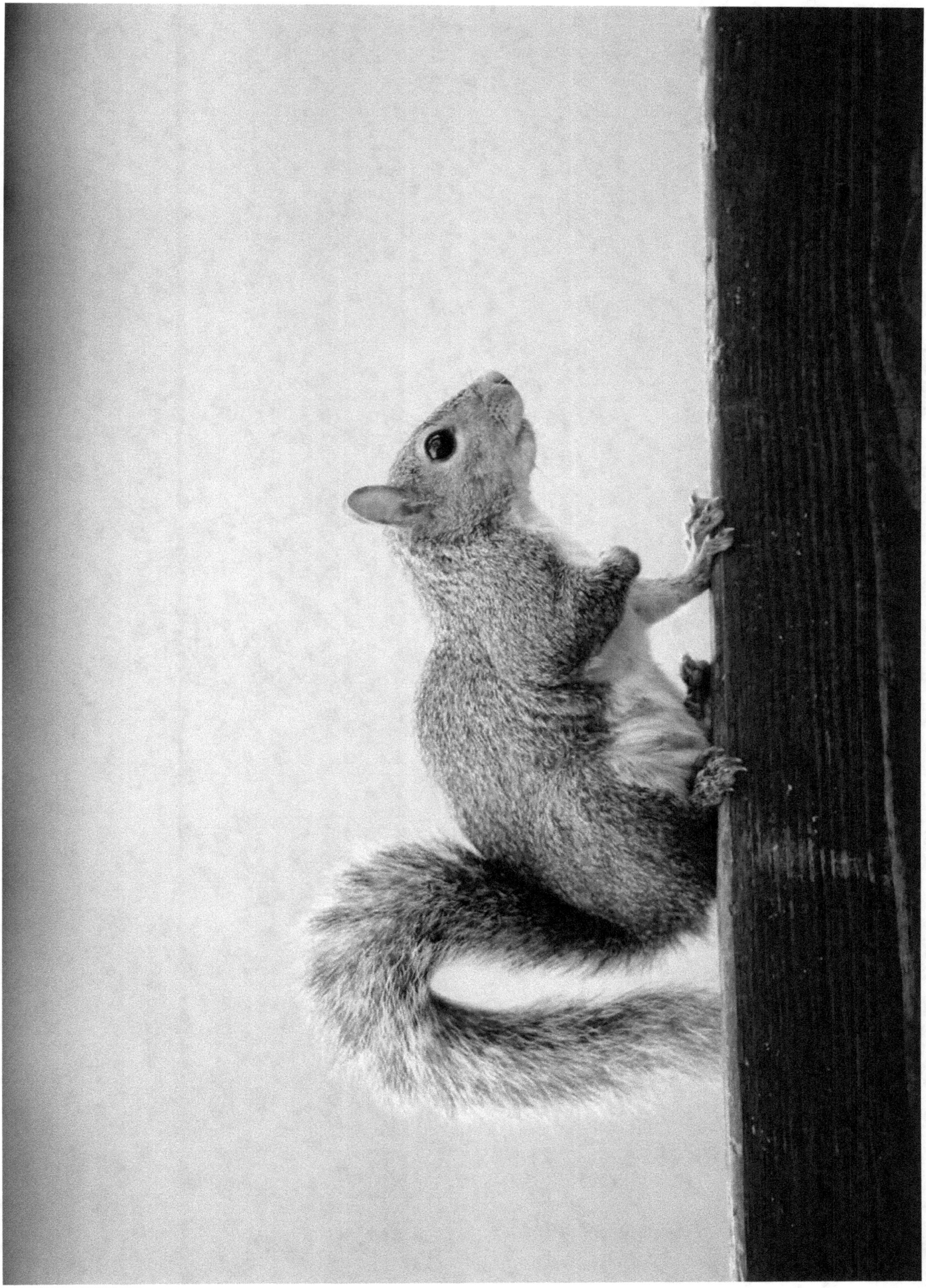

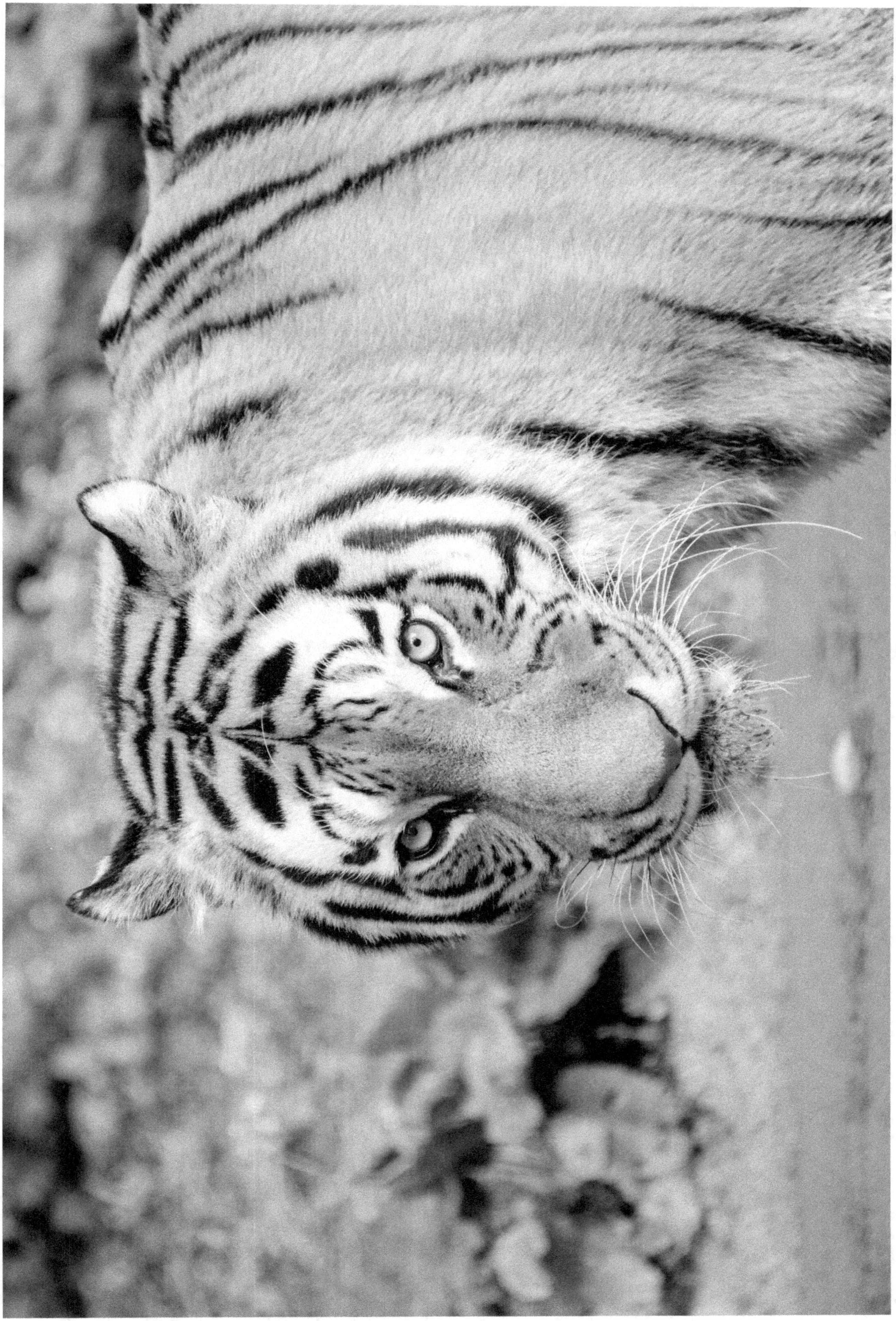

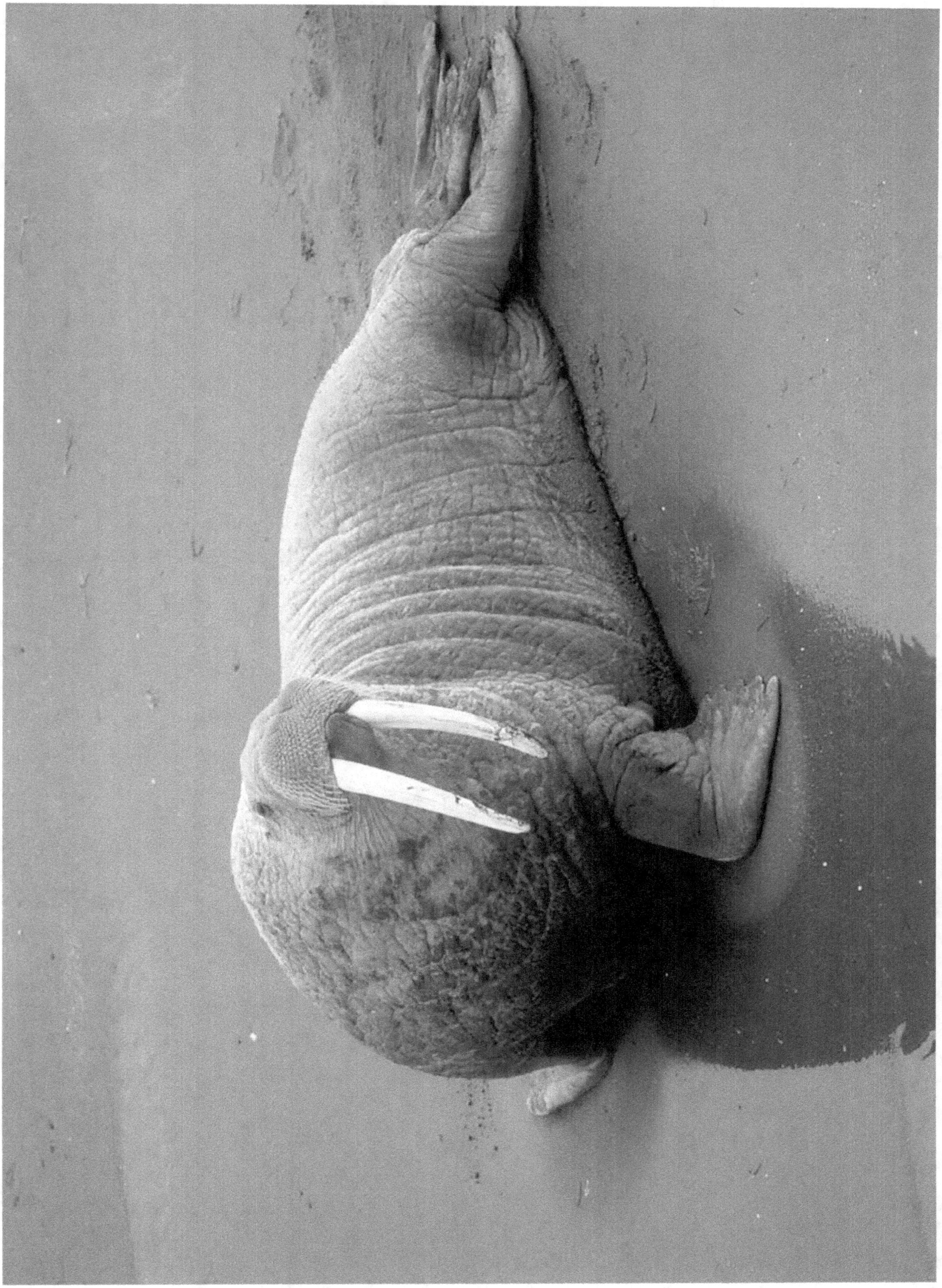

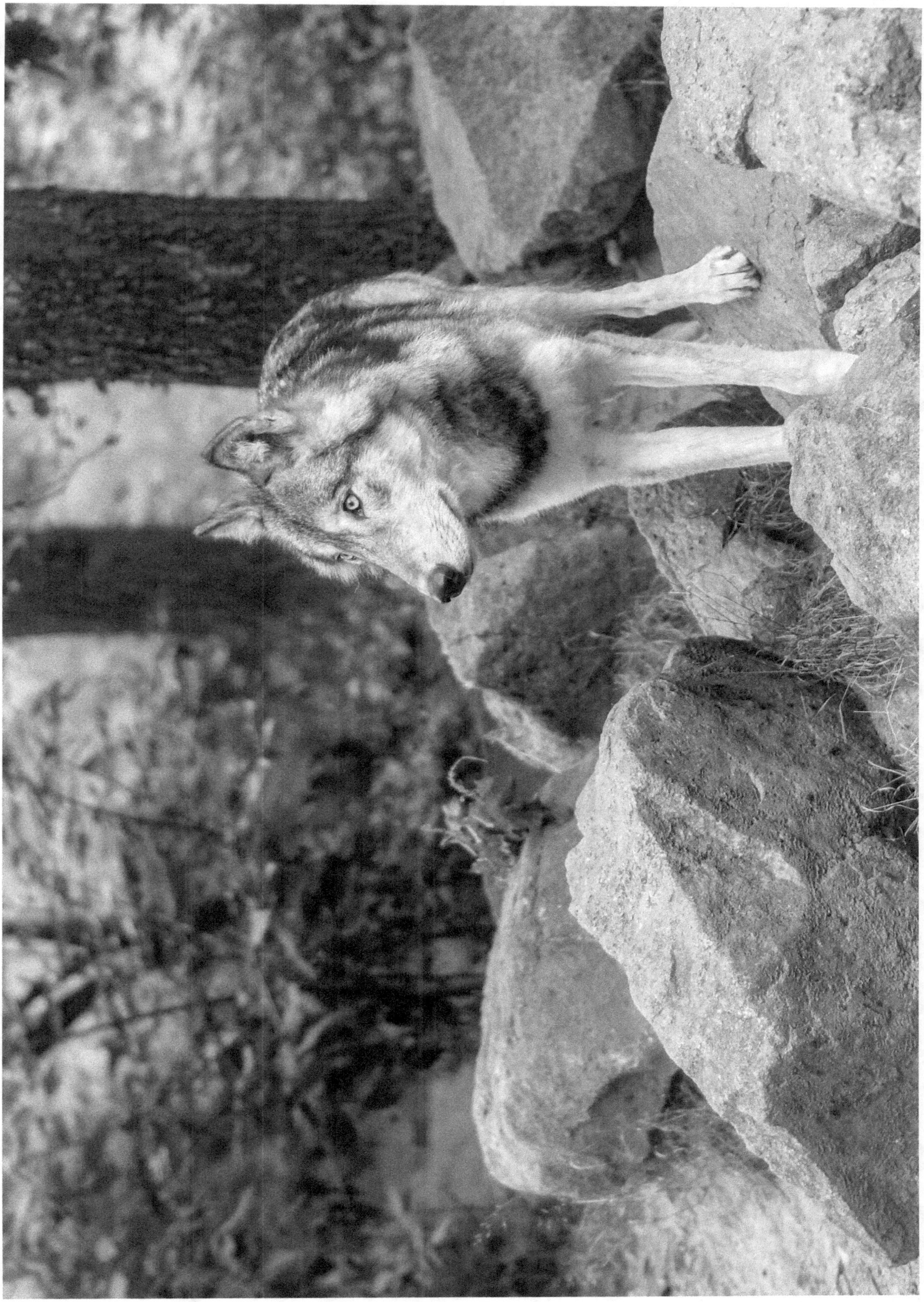

www.ingramcontent.com/pod-product-compliance
Lightning Source LLC
Chambersburg PA
CBHW080909220526
45466CB00011BA/3521
* 9 7 9 8 5 7 5 1 4 3 6 6 6 *